GREAT GALS

INSPIRED IDEAS FOR LIVING A KICK-ASS LIFE

Summer Pierre

A Perigee Book

A PERIGEE BOOK
Published by the Penguin Group
Penguin Group (USA) Inc.
375 Hudson Street, New York, New York 10014, USA

Penguin Group (Canada), 90 Eglinton Avenue East, Suite 700, Toronto, Ontario M4P 2Y3, Canada
(a division of Pearson Penguin Canada Inc.)
Penguin Books Ltd., 80 Strand, London WC2R 0RL, England
Penguin Group Ireland, 25 St. Stephen's Green, Dublin 2, Ireland (a division of Penguin Books Ltd.)
Penguin Group (Australia), 250 Camberwell Road, Camberwell, Victoria 3124, Australia
(a division of Pearson Australia Group Pty. Ltd.)
Penguin Books India Pvt. Ltd., 11 Community Centre, Panchsheel Park, New Delhi—110 017, India
Penguin Group (NZ), 67 Apollo Drive, Rosedale, North Shore 0632, New Zealand
(a division of Pearson New Zealand Ltd.)
Penguin Books (South Africa) (Pty.) Ltd., 24 Sturdee Avenue, Rosebank, Johannesburg 2196, South
    Africa
Penguin Books Ltd., Registered Offices: 80 Strand, London WC2R 0RL, England

While the author has made every effort to provide accurate telephone numbers and Internet
addresses at the time of publication, neither the publisher nor the author assumes any
responsibility for errors or for changes that occur after publication. Further, the publisher does not
have any control over and does not assume any responsibility for author or third-party websites or
their content.

Copyright © 2010 by Summer Pierre
Cover art and design by Summer Pierre
Interior art by Summer Pierre
Interior design by Tiffany Estreicher

First edition: November 2010

Library of Congress Cataloging-in-Publication Data

Pierre, Summer, 1972–
  Great gals : inspired ideas for living a kick-ass life / Summer Pierre— 1st ed.
    p. cm.
  ISBN 978-0-399-53624-3
  1. Women—Biography—Miscellanea. 2. Women—United States—Biography—Miscellanea. I. Title.
  CT 3234.P54 2010
  920.72—dc22   2010025266

PRINTED IN THE UNITED STATES OF AMERICA

10 9 8 7 6 5 4 3 2 1

Most Perigee books are available at special quantity discounts for bulk purchases for sales
promotions, premiums, fund-raising, or educational use. Special books, or book excerpts, can also
be created to fit specific needs. For details, write: Special Markets, Penguin Group (USA) Inc.,
375 Hudson Street, New York, New York 10014.

THIS BOOK IS FOR

JEANNE D. OLIVER
-and-
BETTE JEAN PIERRE

GREAT GALS   MY GRANDMOTHERS

Today is the day to dream of trips to Paris, Listen to Simon & Garfunkle, Karen Ann, Beth orton, draw Comics, Celebrate, Write letters, drink Coffee, Believe in more, read books, buy flowers, take a walk, take a Compliment, eat fresh fruit, let go, kiss your love, love your cat, plan on a cupcake, think up new ideas, Compliment your mom, rock OUT, stare at clouds, take polaroids, laugh out loud, make a list, turn off the Computer, buy new shoes, Shave your legs, talk to muses, feel GREAT, plan a trip, a dream, a way to take over the world, finish Something that is Still unfinished, believe YOU CAN DO IT ALL.

GREAT GALS: an Introduction

As women, we live busy lives, chaotic lives, boring lives, quiet lives, you-name-it lives. But very few of us think we live great lives. Why not? Isn't it the only life we have? Why not make it *great*?

So much of the time we think somebody else has it figured out and is living life more comfortably or confidently. The fact is, that person is thinking the same thing about somebody else (maybe you!).

I have always been inspired by the example of great women. I have pored over their stories and experiences as a way to feel encouraged, to be more daring and inspired, to believe in myself, and also to be a sort of compass, to guide me when I've felt directionless or lost. I have often been surprised at how human these "great" women are. I have sought them out, believing they knew some secret that I didn't, only to find that they also struggle, fear rejection, aren't "discovered" until later in life, are underestimated, or even go see three movies in a row on a beautiful day. Some of them (if not all of them) thought at one time or another: *Why can't I be more like her?* Guess what? You *are* her!

What you have in your hands is not your regular ol' feel-good book or diary. It's a whole lotta greatness: greatness to be planned, greatness to be urged, and greatness to be inspired by. Inside *Great Gals* you will find inspirational quotes, prompts, and ideas to build on your own great life along with scads of pages for you to write down your thoughts and questions and ideas. Along the way there will be famous examples of great gals to keep you going. Please keep going!

make this book your own!

Use it as a daily planner, a diary, a depository for goals, dreams, experiments, ideas—or all of the above! Scribble down sudden brainstorms or use it to doodle with while you're on the phone. Make plans with it, take it to work, paste stickies with random phone numbers in it—all the things that make up your life can go in this book. Most of all, let this book be a reminder that wherever you are, your life is your own. It's whatever you want to make of it. I encourage you to make something of it! I encourage you to make it GREAT.

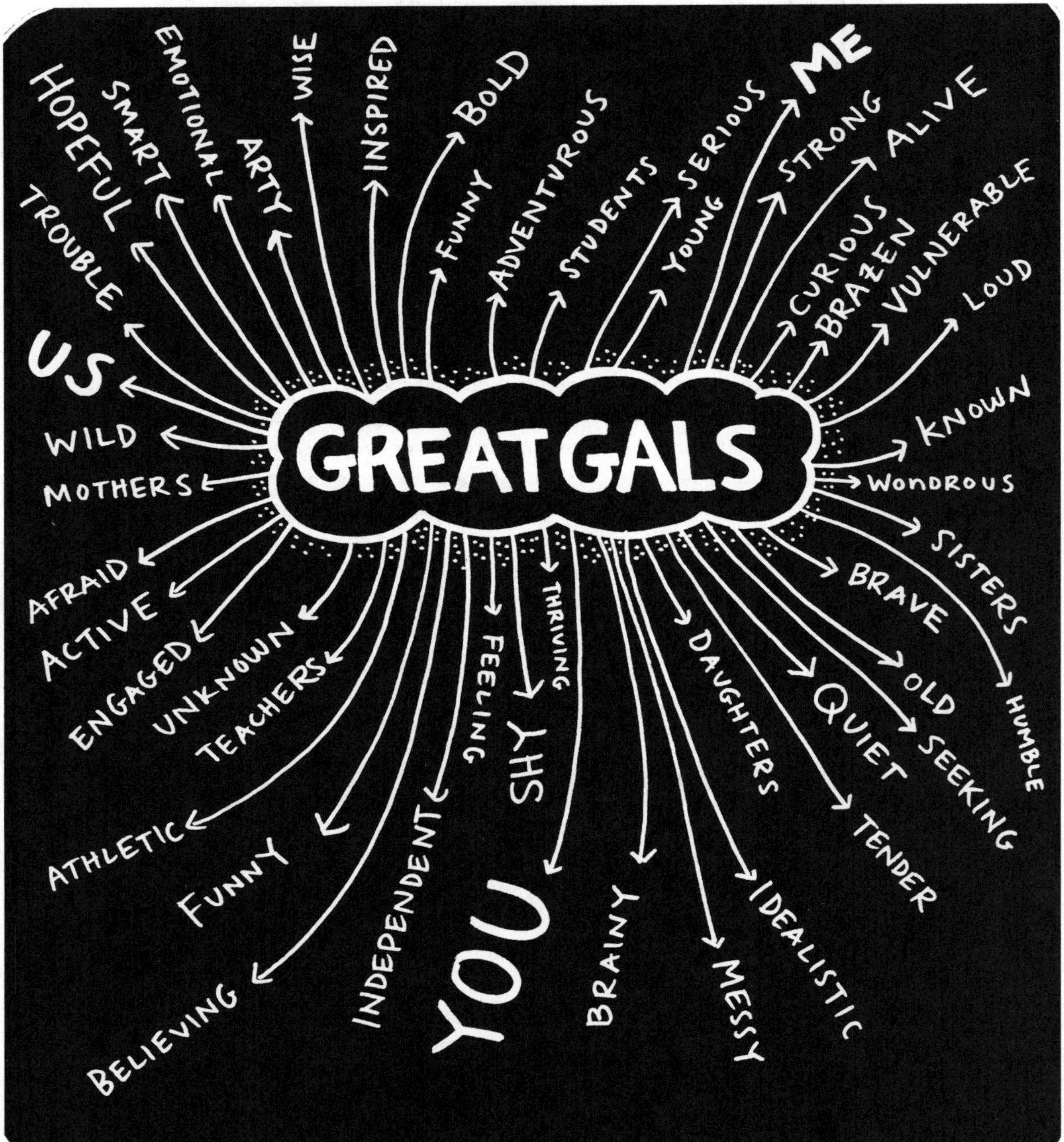
GREAT GALS
TROUBLE
HOPEFUL
SMART
EMOTIONAL
ARTY
WISE
INSPIRED
FUNNY
BOLD
ADVENTUROUS
STUDENTS
YOUNG
SERIOUS
ME
STRONG
CURIOUS
BRAZEN
ALIVE
VULNERABLE
LOUD
US
WILD
MOTHERS
KNOWN
WONDROUS
AFRAID
ACTIVE
ENGAGED
UNKNOWN
TEACHERS
FEELING
SHY
THRIVING
DAUGHTERS
SISTERS
BRAVE
OLD
QUIET
SEEKING
HUMBLE
ATHLETIC
FUNNY
INDEPENDENT
YOU
BRAINY
MESSY
IDEALISTIC
TENDER
BELIEVING

CYNDI LAUPER!

Great Gals are underestimated!

Probably one of the most underrated pop rock artists today, Cynthia Anne Stephanie Lauper was born in Queens, New York, in 1953. At an early age she discovered music and taught herself to play the guitar and write her own songs. She spent many years singing in cover bands and writing original songs with her band, Blue Angel, before she was signed as a solo artist to Portrait Records and recorded her 1984 smash-hit album, *She's So Unusual*. The record label was skeptical of her songwriting talents and wouldn't let her record any of her own material. They finally relented when the producer suggested the album needed one more song, and she recorded "Time After Time," cowritten with musician Rob Hyman. It would go on to hit number one on both Billboard and Adult Contemporary charts, as well as be recorded and covered by more than a hundred other artists. This was not the first time she was underestimated, nor would it be the last. Years after her music stopped hitting the top 40 charts, she would prove herself to be a gifted actress, winning an Emmy for her recurring guest spot on the sitcom *Mad About You*.

ESTEEMED ESTIMATION

IS THERE ANYTHING YOU HAVE BEEN TOLD YOU COULD NOT DO?

FINISH THESE SENTENCES:

IF GIVEN THE CHANCE I KNOW I COULD...

SECRETLY, I KNOW I AM...

When I sing I don't feel like it's me. I feel I am fabulous, like I'm ten feet tall. I am the greatest. I am the strongest... I am whoever I want to be. — Cyndi Lauper

Ingrid Bergman

Great Gals follow their hearts!

Swedish actress and American film icon Ingrid Bergman was born in Stockholm in 1915. As a teenager, she appeared as an extra in Swedish films and went on to study at the Royal Dramatic Theatre school in Stockholm. In 1936, she landed the starring role in the Swedish film *Intermezzo* that attracted the American film producer David O. Selznick, who immediately cast her in the American remake. It was through Selznick's direction that Bergman became a sensation in such iconic films as *Casablanca*, *Notorious*, and *Gaslight*. In 1950, at the height of her fame, she shocked and soured audiences when she openly had an affair with Italian filmmaker Roberto Rossellini while they were both still married to other people. When she became pregnant, she was blackballed by the media. Never to be deterred, she returned to Europe, married Rossellini, and continued to act in Italian films, living in exile from Hollywood. It wasn't until 1956, when she appeared in the film *Anastasia* and won her second Academy Award, that American audiences seemed to "forgive" her and she resumed her Hollywood career. She never apologized for her actions and always remained true to what was in her heart. She died from cancer on her sixty-seventh birthday.

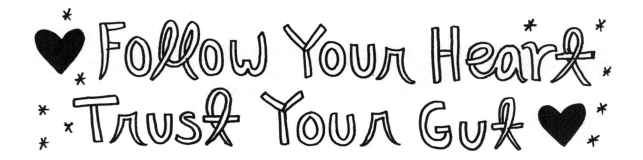

Follow Your Heart
Trust Your Gut

HAVE YOU EVER WANTED TO DO SOMETHING THAT SEEMED "UNPOPULAR" OR "RISKY"? WHAT WAS IT?

EXAMPLE: START OR QUIT SCHOOL, MOVE TO ANOTHER TOWN, LIKE SOMEONE, ETC.

WHAT WERE SOME OF THE OPPOSING VOICES AGAINST THAT CHOICE- EITHER FROM YOURSELF OR SOMEONE ELSE?

DID YOU LISTEN? WHY OR WHY NOT?

IS THERE SOMETHING YOU DID DO DESPITE DISCOURAGING FEEDBACK?

HOW DID THAT FEEL?

WHAT WAS THE OUTCOME?

IF THERE IS SOMETHING YOU REGRET NOT DOING BECAUSE YOU WERE TOO SCARED OR SOMEONE TALKED YOU OUT OF IT, IS THERE A WAY YOU CAN RECLAIM IT? SOMETIMES JUST MAKING A COMMITMENT TO LISTENING TO YOURSELF FIRST CAN BE ENOUGH. SOMETIMES TAKING LATE ACTION IS BETTER THAN NOTHING. EXPLORE IDEAS HERE:

I have had a wonderful life. I have never regretted what I did. I regret things I didn't do... I was given courage, a sense of adventure, and a little bit of humor. I don't think anyone has the right to intrude in your life, but they do. – Ingrid Bergman

Everyday Acts of Power

BE BOLD! BE YOU! DARE TO DO IT!

Risk Being Seen
ENTER A CONTEST! HANG A PICTURE IN A PUBLIC PLACE! ASK SOMEONE OUT ON A DATE!

Step out of Fear
START A CONVERSATION WITH YOUR NEIGHBORS. COMPLIMENT A STRANGER, WALK DOWN THE STREET SINGING OUT LOUD.

Level The Playing Field
WRITE A LETTER (WITH STAMPS & ENVELOPE) TO SOMEONE YOU GREATLY ADMIRE! (THEY HAVE MAIL-BOXES!)

Question Your Assumptions
WHAT IS ONE SMALL THING YOU TELL YOURSELF YOU CAN'T DO? THROW A FRISBEE? WRITE A POEM? WEAR A BIKINI? TRY IT NOW.

Challenge Your Routine
FOR ONE WEEK: TURN OFF YOUR TV! WATCH THE SUNRISE! WALK TO WORK! GO OUT DANCING!

Empower Others
MAKE SOME SANDWICHES AND GIVE THEM TO THE HOMELESS! OFFER TO DO SOMEONE'S LAUNDRY OR TO COOK THEM A MEAL!

Be Proud of Yourself
WRITE A LIST OF ALL THE THINGS YOU'VE DONE THAT YOU'RE PROUD OF. PRIDE IS POWER!

Dazzle Yourself
GET DRESSED UP AND TAKE YOUR FABULOUS SELF OUT ON THE TOWN! WHAT ARE YOU WAITING FOR?

Great Gals fail better!

Margaret Cho was born in San Francisco in 1968. She began doing stand-up comedy at an early age, touring the United States as a teenager and making people laugh about her Korean family life. When she was offered her own TV show based on her material, she thought she had really made it as an actress. The experience turned out to be a disaster. Producers pressured Cho to lose thirty pounds in three weeks, and she ended up in the hospital. Cho's often crass and edgy comedy was also watered down to fit the sitcom mold. Then, due to lukewarm reviews and poor audience ratings, the show was canceled after just one season. This could be considered a great failure in Cho's career, but it turned out to be a turning point. She once said, "It was a good experience as far as finding myself, knowing who I was and what direction I wanted to take with my comedy." Cho would go onto use this experience to create the smash-hit one-woman show, film, and bestselling book *I'm the One That I Want*. It garnered her rave reviews, fame, and great respect. She has continued to evolve and expand her work doing stand-up, writing books, performing burlesque, and performing music.

FAIL ★ BETTER ★ NOW

Sometimes our "failures" can be the gateway to a life we never imagined

REGRET OR FAILURE:

WHY IT HURTS:

WHAT CAN YOU DO ABOUT IT:

WHAT IS ONE POSITIVE THING THAT CAME FROM IT:

I'm not going to die because I failed as someone else. I'm going to succeed as myself.
— Margaret Cho

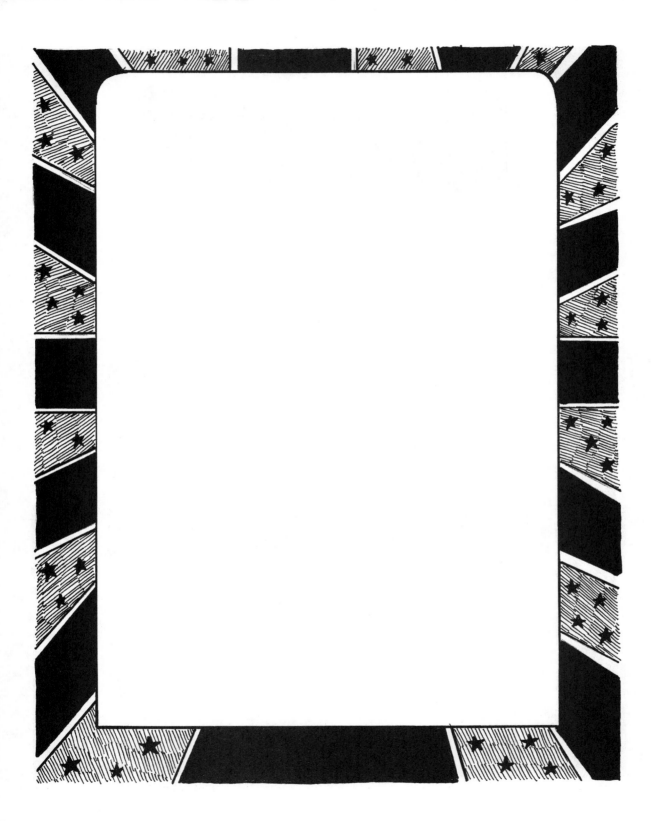

NEVER LET GO OF THAT FIERY SAD-NESS CALLED DESIRE. /// PATTI SMITH

STRESS TEST

EXAMPLE: BOSS YELLING

WHAT STRESSES YOU OUT?

EXAMPLE: A GLASS OF WINE

WHAT RELAXES YOU?

EXAMPLE: BEING LATE FOR SOMETHING

WHAT RATTLES YOU?

EXAMPLE: THE SMELL OF BAKING

WHAT GIVES YOU A SENSE OF WELL-BEING?

EXAMPLE: MONEY FEARS

WHAT IS BUGGING YOU RIGHT NOW?

EXAMPLE: I HAVE FOOD AT HOME

HOW ARE YOU SAFE IN THIS MOMENT?

EXAMPLE: DID I SAY THE WRONG THING?

WORRIES

EXAMPLE: I TRUST THINGS WILL WORK OUT

AFFIRMATIONS

You Are Always on Your Way To A Miracle.   — SARK

BETSEY JOHNSON

Great Gals have their own sense of style!

Betsey Johnson was born in Wethersfield, Connecticut, in 1942. As a girl, she studied dance and found her lifelong inspiration for theatrical, moving clothes through the costumes she wore. In 1964, she won a coveted guest editorship at *Mademoiselle* (previous winners include Sylvia Plath and Joan Didion), which launched her fashion career. She opened her first boutique called Betsey Bunki Nini in 1969; at the time, she was part of the Andy Warhol Factory scene. Edie Sedgwick was her house model and her clothes were often seen on the Velvet Underground's John Cale (Johnson's then boyfriend). After nearly a decade of designing for other labels such as Alley Cat and Alvin Duskin, Johnson started her own label, Betsey Johnson, which has been celebrated for its colorful, playful, and ever-evolving line for more than thirty years. The honoree of several lifetime achievement awards, Johnson has remained an inspiration for ceaseless creativity and innovation in an industry known for its fickle nature. She continues to expand her line and remains an exciting and vibrant figure in fashion.

FASHIONABLY YOU

- I'VE always LOVED TO WEAR...

- IT makes ME feel...
- SECRETLY, I hate WEARING...

- IT makes ME feel...

- IF I COULD get away WITH IT, I'D love TO WEAR...

- I WOULD NEVER BE caught DEAD IN...

- SECRETLY, I'VE always LIKED THE LOOK OF...

- I FEEL powerful WHEN I WEAR...

- I FEEL beautiful WHEN I WEAR...

- IF I COULD ONLY own ONE ITEM OF clothing IT WOULD BE...

Girls do not dress for boys. They dress for themselves and, of course, each other. If girls dressed for boys, they'd just walk around naked at all times. — Betsey Johnson

ELLA FITZGERALD

Great Gals don't know what they are Capable of!

Hailed as the First Lady of Song, Ella Jane Fitzgerald was born in Newport News, Virginia, in 1917. In the 1920s, Fitzgerald and her mother, Tempie, moved to Yonkers, New York. When Fitzgerald was fifteen, her mother died suddenly due to complications from a car accident. The loss was devastating to Fitzgerald, who started skipping school and running away from home and eventually went to a reform school. Then in 1934, at the age of seventeen, she entered the Apollo Theater's amateur night, planning to perform as a dancer, but quickly changed her mind when she saw a dance duo compete. Without any forethought she decided to sing and ended up winning over the audience with her incredible voice. It was the beginning of a career that would span sixty years and give her the reputation as one of the greatest interpreters of the American songbook. Not bad for someone with absolutely no formal training. She continued to perform until her death in 1996.

The Time is Now

- ~~THIS YEAR~~ Today I WANT TO:

- ~~THIS YEAR~~ Today I PLAN TO:

Today

- ~~THIS YEAR~~ I CAN:

Today

- ~~THIS YEAR~~ I AM:

The only thing better than singing is more singing. - Ella Fitzgerald

Don't be afraid
that your
life will
end, be afraid
that it will
never begin.
- Anonymous

Great Gals are late bloomers!

Painter, writer, and Canadian national treasure Emily Carr was born in 1871. She showed an early spirit of determination and adventure by refusing to ride sidesaddle, choosing not to get married, and traveling on sketching trips to remote villages of the Canadian West. For fifteen years, she studied art in London, Paris, and San Francisco, then she all but stopped creating art while she made a living running a boarding house. At the age of fifty-five, she took a course in creative writing and began writing the stories that would become her first book, *Klee Wyck*. Around the same time, she resumed painting. The works she produced between the ages of fifty-six and seventy-one would go on to make her the most recognized and treasured Canadian artist and writer.

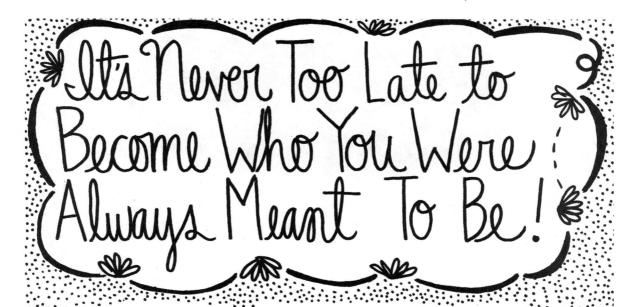

It's Never Too Late to Become Who You Were Always Meant To Be!

FINISH THESE SENTENCES:

∽ SECRETLY, I HAVE ALWAYS WANTED TO...

∽ SECRETLY, I BELIEVE I AM GOOD AT...

∽ SECRETLY, I MISS DOING...

Something has called out of
Somewhere and something in
me is trying to answer.
   - Emily Carr

yes, THIS IS
Lucille Ball

Great Gals try and try again!

Lucille Désirée Ball was born in 1911 in Jamestown, New York. At sixteen, she came home after studying for two weeks at the John Murray Anderson School for the Dramatic Arts in New York City, where teachers told her that she had no future in performing. She returned to New York City two years later, determined to prove them wrong, only to be stricken with a debilitating case of rheumatoid arthritis. Two years later, she landed bit parts in Broadway shows. In 1933, she relocated to Hollywood and, over the next fifteen years, she gained notoriety for the numerous B feature flicks she acted in. It wasn't until 1948 when she landed one of the leads in the radio comedy *My Favorite Husband* that her brilliant comedic timing was revealed. When CBS asked her to develop it for television, she insisted that her real-life husband, Cuban entertainer Desi Arnaz, play her husband on the show. CBS was reluctant to cast Arnaz, not convinced that audiences would believe an all-American girl would be married to a Cuban. To prove them wrong, Arnaz and Ball took their show on tour, selling out theaters across the country. The sitcom, *I Love Lucy*, premiered on TV in October 1951, running a successful nine years and launching Ball into superstardom. She remains one of the most iconic comedic actresses of all time.

How are you brave?

How do you hide?

IN what ways do you try?

I'm not funny. What I am is brave.
   - Lucille Ball

Great Gals challenge assumptions!

Billie Jean King (née Moffitt) was born in 1943 in Long Beach, California, to a conservative Methodist family. At age eleven, she began taking free tennis lessons at Houghton Park in Long Beach. Her fierce competitive nature was detected early, when her mother picked her up from practice and King announced, "I am going to be number one." She made good on her promise, winning several tournaments throughout the late 1960s and early '70s. At this time, she lobbied for women to receive equal payment in tournament prize money as men, and won. She also helped create and promote the first women's professional tennis title tour, Virginia Slims. Despite her championships and accomplishments, she is best known for winning the Battle of the Sexes against Bobby Riggs in 1973. Riggs, a tennis star in the 1930s and '40s, took to publicly denouncing women's tennis as inferior and making claims that he could beat any of the top women tennis players. After accepting a lucrative offer, King agreed to play Riggs. King has said of the event, "I thought it would set us back fifty years if I didn't win that match. It would ruin the women's [tennis] tour and affect all women's self-esteem." Her win was said to have had a major impact not only on women's tennis but also on the women's movement.

QUESTION YOUR ASSUMPTIONS

IT'S TIME TO *Risk* YOUR IDEAS ABOUT YOURSELF!

① WHAT DO YOU BELIEVE YOU ARE NOT GOOD AT? PLAYING POOL? WRITING POEMS? WRITE IT HERE:

② WHAT IS SOMETHING YOU WOULD "NEVER" DO? GO SKINNY DIPPING? WEAR HIGH HEELS? WRITE IT HERE:

③ NOW PICK ONE ITEM FROM EITHER LIST AND DO IT! HOW DID IT FEEL? WRITE IT DOWN HERE:

You will be surprised by yourself!

The main thing is to care. Care very hard, even if it is only a game you are playing.
— Billie Jean King

"I walk ahead of myself in perpetual expectancy of miracles."

Anaïs Nin

Great Gals explore the wisdom of their hearts!

Anaïs Nin was born just outside of Paris in 1903. When she was eleven years old, her composer father abandoned the family, causing her mother to move with Nin and her brothers to the United States. On the boat to New York, Nin began keeping a diary, a practice she would continue passionately for the rest of her life. In 1923, she married Hugh Guiler but would have many love affairs—among them the writer Henry Miller, who inspired and encouraged her writing for more than thirty years. She would go on to write many surrealist novels and collections of erotic stories, but it was her ardent and beautiful diaries that would eventually make her name. The journals, first published in 1966, depict not only a life lived among noteworthy and famous writers and individuals, but a deep and personal inquiry of female sexuality, creativity, and experience. Her diary's example has inspired generations of women to follow suit and explore the wisdom of their own paths through personal writing.

YOU ARE WISE

FINISH THIS SENTENCE:

NOBODY TOLD ME...

The personal life deeply lived always expands into truths beyond itself.
       — Anaïs Nin

Emily Dickinson

Great Gals keep their own Company!

Emily Dickinson was born in Amherst, Massachusetts, in 1830. When she was seventeen, she went to Mount Holyoke Female Seminary, but returned home a year later, rarely to leave again. At home, she spent her time reading widely, gardening, and having ardent and prolific correspondences with several individuals. She became known as an eccentric in her hometown, wearing only white and seldom leaving her home and, later, her room. She also wrote poems constantly, a number of which were published in her lifetime. However, her own siblings did not even know the extent to which she wrote. After her death in 1886, forty hand-bound volumes of nearly 1,800 poems were discovered among her things. Many of her poems deal with longing and isolation, death, and immortality, subjects also covered in her correspondence. She is considered one of the greatest poets in American history.

WHAT ARE SOME OF YOUR GUILTY PLEASURES? DO YOU LOVE TO EAT IN BED? WATCH <u>COPS</u> AND DRINK BEER? WHAT DO YOU LOVE TO DO WHEN NO ONE IS LOOKING?

SOME IDEAS FOR ALONE ACTIVITIES: COOKING YOUR FAVORITE CHILDHOOD MEAL (AND EATING IT!) • GIVE YOURSELF A HOME SPA: LIGHT CANDLES, TAKE A BATH, AND PAINT YOUR NAILS • EXPLORE A TOWN YOU'VE ALWAYS WANTED TO GO TO • SHOPPING • LONG WALKS WITH HEADPHONES!

Dwell in possibility.
- Emily Dickinson

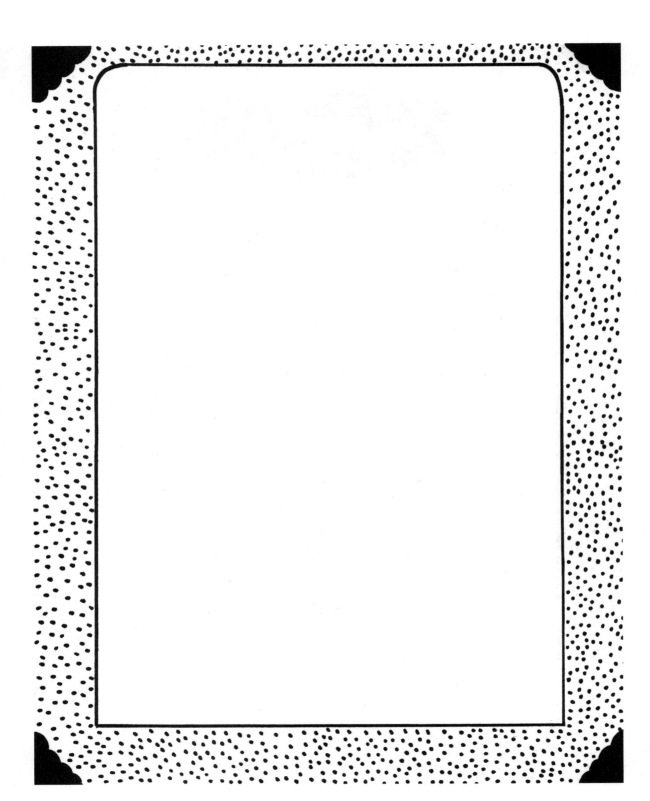

OH, FOR THE LOVE OF YOU!

IDEAS FOR A SPECIAL NIGHT FOR ①!

What would your ideal date be? WHERE WOULD YOU GO? WHAT WOULD YOU DO? HOW ABOUT TRYING IT ON YOURSELF?

WHAT A CATCH!

Wear something Fabulous! Dress up! WHEN YOU FEEL BEAUTIFUL IT GIVES YOU CONFIDENCE! PUT ON THAT SPECIAL NUMBER YOU KNOW YOU LOOK GOOD IN! GO OUT WITH THE FEELING: I AM SOMETHING!

Send Yourself Flowers — Better than Just buying!

SPECIAL DELIVERY!

OH, THANK YOU!

Some helpful items to bring with you: JOURNAL WITH PENS TO WRITE WITH * A BOOK TO READ * A CAMERA TO RECORD YOUR ADVENTURE * LOVING THOUGHTS TO YOURSELF — IT TAKES GUTS TO BE OUT ON YOUR OWN!

Places You MIGHT GO:

DANCING!

GALLERY HOPPING!

A MOVIE ESPECIALLY ONE YOU HAVE SECRETLY BEEN DYING TO SEE! P.S. BUY THE WORKS — POPCORN, SODA, CANDY!

TRY A NEW RESTAURANT

BOOK EVENT!

THEATER

ANY EVENTS YOU HAVE BEEN WANTING TO GO!

HAVE THE TIME OF YOUR LIFE!

At Last, Etta James

Great Gals rise above ruin!

Jamesetta Hawkins was born in Los Angeles in 1938. While living in San Francisco, at the age of fourteen, she formed the doo-wop group the Peaches and auditioned for the bandleader Johnny Otis. Without her mother's consent, James went down to Los Angeles to record a song called "The Wallflower" in Otis's studio. It went to number two on the R & B charts in 1955. The Peaches soon disbanded, but James went on to record and tour on her own, releasing several singles and eventually signing with Chess Records. In the 1960s, she recorded such hits as "All I Could Do Is Cry" and her signature song, "At Last." Throughout most of her life, Etta James battled heroin addiction, which resulted in legal troubles and several hospitalizations. Her addiction deeply affected her career and, by the 1980s, it was widely considered that her career was over. Then in 1994, she released a tribute album to her hero Billie Holiday, which won her the Grammy Award for Best Jazz Vocal Performance, and began her climb back into the critical limelight. That year, she was inducted into the Rock and Roll Hall of Fame and began performing again at prestigious festivals like the Monterey Jazz Festival. In 2004, *Rolling Stone* named her 62 on their list of 100 Greatest Artists of All Time.

WHAT ARE YOU LEARNING?

WE ARE ALWAYS LEARNING SOMETHING IN THE SCHOOL OF LIFE!

ABOUT YOUR JOB	ABOUT YOUR HOME	ABOUT WHAT YOU LIKE

ABOUT WHAT YOU DON'T LIKE	ABOUT SOMEONE YOU KNOW	ABOUT ANYTHING

WHAT WOULD YOU LIKE TO LEARN?

A NEW RECIPE? THE TWO-STEP? WHAT IT'S LIKE TO KISS SOMEBODY IN ARUBA? WRITE IDEAS HERE:

I sing the songs that people need to hear. - Etta James

WE MAY encounter MANY DEFEATS, BUT WE must NOT be DEFEATED.
— MAYA Angelou

Ani DiFranco

Great Gals are independent!

Born in Buffalo, New York, in 1970, Ani DiFranco began performing at the age of nine. By the time she was nineteen, she had recorded her first CD and written more than a hundred songs. With her original guitar strumming/picking style, intensely honest and often political songwriting, and years of steadfast touring, she has garnered one of the largest and most dedicated followings of any folk musician. In 1989, she started her own label, Righteous Babe Records, to produce and release her albums, which to date number more than twenty. DiFranco has spoken openly against the major-label system of the music industry. Without commercial airplay, hit singles, or major-label support, she has carved out a unique and powerful presence in rock and folk music. As a result of her hardworking and independent vision, DiFranco has expanded Righteous Babe Records to release albums by other likeminded artists and to provide the Buffalo community with a performance space created out of an old Methodist church. She remains a powerful feminist icon.

You Are the One That You Want

WHO DO YOU ADMIRE AND WHY? LIST ALL CHARACTERISTICS HERE:

HOW MANY OF THESE SAME CHARACTERISTICS CAN BE USED TO ALSO DESCRIBE YOU?

LIST THEM HERE:

NEXT TIME YOU CATCH YOURSELF YEARNING FOR WHAT SOMEONE ELSE ENCOMPASSES, THINKING "OH, SHE'S SO TALENTED," OR "HE'S SO BRAVE," STOP!

POSSESS THESE BELIEFS FOR YOURSELF: SAY "I AM SO TALENTED!" OR "I AM SO BRAVE!"

WRITE IT OUT HERE:

WRITE A LIST OF THINGS YOU ARE PROUD TO HAVE DONE. PRIDE IS POWER!

EXTRA CREDIT: FIND THE PERSON YOU ADMIRE'S SNAIL MAIL ADDRESS AND WRITE THEM A LETTER! DO NOT USE E-MAIL— IT'S TOO EASY TO IGNORE! WRITING THEM A REAL NOTE OR POSTCARD LEVELS THE PLAYING FIELD. SUDDENLY, THEY ARE A REAL, LIVING PERSON WITH A MAILBOX! WHO KNOWS? YOU MIGHT JUST GET A LETTER BACK! YOU ARE A REAL, LIVING PERSON WITH A MAILBOX!

I'd rather be able to face myself in the bathroom mirror than be rich and famous. – Ani DiFranco

I AM NOT MYSELF; I AM THE POTENTIAL OF MYSELF.

— ANNA DEAVERE SMITH

AMY SEDARIS

Great Gals do it all!

Amy Sedaris was born the fourth of six children in upstate New York in 1961. At an early age, she would outfit herself in costumes and do impressions of neighbors and teachers. Her favorite gifts as a kid were wigs and prosthetics. In her twenties, she studied and performed with Chicago's famed Second City troupe along with such comedic luminaries as Steven Colbert and Paul Dinello. Her early work in sketch comedy displayed her gifts for creating absurd, often grotesque, and funny characters. She has said of her creative process: "If I am creating something for myself, then I want to have fun. I like to play unattractive people who think they're pretty. You can do what you want, but I prefer to look interesting." This is probably best displayed in her character Jerri Blank, the unlovable ex-prostitute who returns to high school on the cult favorite TV show and movie *Strangers with Candy*. The spirit of fun and interesting can also be detected in Sedaris's fledgling cheese ball and cupcake business, and in her book on entertaining, *I Like You: Hospitality Under the Influence*, which came out in 2006 to wide acclaim. She continues to mine the absurd, living with her pet rabbit, Dusty, and married to her imaginary husband, Glenn.

WHAT ARE SOME THINGS YOU K<u>NOW</u>
YOU ARE GOOD AT?

WHICH ONES HAVE YOU BEEN T<u>OLD</u>
YOU WERE GOOD AT?

WHICH ONES DO YOU JUST <u>FEEL</u> YOU ARE GOOD AT?

WHAT <u>TELLS</u> YOU YOU ARE GOOD AT THEM?

WHICH SKILLS DO YOU VALUE MORE? WHY?

GET OUT OF THAT BOX!

I like to do it all. I think that's people's problem with me. They can't put me in a box, and when they do put me in a box, I want to get out of that box. —Amy Sedaris

ALL THAT IS REALLY NECESSARY FOR SURVIVAL OF THE FITTEST, IT SEEMS, IS AN INTEREST IN LIFE, GOOD, BAD, OR PECULIAR.

— GRACE PALEY

Dolly Parton

Great Gals stick to their guns!

The fourth of twelve children, Dolly Rebecca Parton was born in Sevier County, Tennessee, in 1946. When she was seven years old, she was given her first guitar and, at age ten, was performing on local TV and radio. By eighteen, she had moved to Nashville to live with her uncle, Bill Owens, to try her hand at music. In 1967, she got her first charted hit, "Dumb Blonde." She was thrilled when Elvis Presley asked to cover one of her songs in 1974, but soon discovered that he would only do so if she handed over the publishing rights. She refused and never lived to regret it. Her fame climbed steadily in the 1970s and throughout the '80s, when she starred in movies and opened her own amusement park, Dollywood. In a career spanning forty years, her colorful image as a big-breasted blonde has sometimes overshadowed her tremendous gift for songwriting; her songs have been covered by everyone from Whitney Houston to the White Stripes. As she has said, "I look just like the girls next door . . . if you happen to live next door to an amusement park." Her most recent efforts have been to compose the songs for the stage musical version of the movie 9 to 5 and to launch a national literacy project. A prolific songwriter, she continues to be a legendary performer and presence.

Speak Easy

IF I LET MY VULNERABILITY SPEAK, IT WOULD SAY:

IF I LET MY COURAGE SPEAK, IT WOULD SAY:

IF I LET MY AMBITION SPEAK, IT WOULD SAY:

IF I LET MY JEALOUSY SPEAK, IT WOULD SAY:

IF I LET MY STRENGTH SPEAK, IT WOULD SAY:

I'm not offended by all the dumb blonde jokes because I know I'm not dumb... and I also know that I'm not blonde.
— Dolly Parton

Julia Child

Great Gals follow their joy!

Julia Carolyn McWilliams was born in Pasadena, California, in 1912. During World War II, she worked in various administrative capacities for the Office of Strategic Services, where she met her husband, Paul Child. Paul, who had lived abroad and developed a taste for exotic and gourmet foods, introduced Julia to the world of culinary delights. After the war, Paul was stationed in Paris, and Julia, now a housewife, craved a direction of her own. She decided to follow her delight of French food and study at Le Cordon Bleu. "I was thirty-two when I started cooking," she said. "Up until then, I just ate." Julia Child would go on to introduce the pleasures and techniques of French cuisine to the American public, and change the culinary world forever.

HAPPY HAPPY

WHAT GIVES YOU JOY?

FOLLOW YOUR JOY

JOY · JOY · JOY

Find Something you're passionate about and keep tremendously interested in it.
– Julia Child

Nikki Giovanni

Nikki Giovanni was born Yolande Cornelia Giovanni in Knoxville, Tennessee, in 1943, and was raised in Lincoln Heights, an all-black suburb of Cincinnati, Ohio. Her powerful poetry has covered both the political and the personal, garnering her high praise and bestseller status. Her first two collections of poems, *Black Feeling, Black Talk* and *Black Judgement*, were self-published. As she said, "Like a lot of artists, I have this great fear of rejection, and I really couldn't see that the poetry establishment was going to be any great lover of my work." *Black Feeling, Black Talk* went on to be a large seller, way beyond what Giovanni could supply, and was bootlegged and distributed widely, garnering the attention of the publisher William Morrow. William Morrow offered a generous advance for the two books (unheard of for poetry), and Giovanni was soon on her way to becoming the Grammy-nominated, award-winning, and legendary poet she is known as today.

REJECT REJECTION

WHEN DOES FEAR OF REJECTION STOP YOU? WHEN TRYING NEW THINGS? MAKING THE FIRST MOVE?

IF THERE WAS NO POSSIBLE WAY YOU COULD FAIL, WHAT WOULD YOU TRY?

ACCEPT YOURSELF FIRST! DO NOT PRE-REJECT YOURSELF! TAKING THE ABOVE DESIRES—WHAT IS ONE SMALL ACTION YOU CAN TAKE TOWARD THAT DREAM/GOAL/IDEA?

I really don't think life is about the I-could-have-beens. Life is only about the I-tried-to-do. I don't mind the failure but I can't imagine that I'd forgive myself if I didn't try.   — Nikki Giovanni

Isadora Duncan

Great Gals are generous with their gifts!

Isadora Duncan was born in San Francisco in 1877 and raised in a house filled with creativity and art. Her mother's passion for literature, music, and art deeply influenced Duncan's enthusiasm for arts education. She began dancing as a young girl, teaching classes early on, and performing in various productions. While performing in London and Paris to private high-society ladies, her popularity began to grow. Always independent, she had two children out of wedlock. When the children were killed tragically in an accident, she decided to devote herself to the dance schools she had opened for poor children. She would eventually go on to adopt six of her students and perform with them throughout Europe. Unfortunately, her life would be cut tragically short when, in 1927, one of her flowing scarves got caught in the axle of a car she was riding in, strangling her.

Living Generously

FINISH THESE SENTENCES:

▸ IF I LIVED IN A GENEROUS WORLD, I WOULD...

▸ IF I WAS MORE GENEROUS WITH MYSELF, I COULD...

➲ IF I WAS MORE GENEROUS WITH OTHERS, I WOULD...

➲ WAYS IN WHICH I AM GENEROUS ARE...

YOUR GENEROSITY IS A GIFT

The finest inheritance you can give to a child is to allow it to make its own way, completely on its own feet.
— Isadora Duncan

MY AMBITION WAS TO LIVE LIKE MUSIC.

— MARY GAITSKILL

"When I am done with my plan, when I am very old, hopefully there will be a little more space for people living with profound doubt to tell their stories in all different mediums."

Miranda July

Great Gals start their own Communities!

Artist, filmmaker, and writer Miranda July was born in 1974 and grew up in Berkeley, California. She attended UC Santa Cruz with the intention of becoming a filmmaker, but found the program so disappointing that she quit and moved to Portland, Oregon, where the female indie do-it-yourself scene was taking off. In order to feel less lonely, she started a video chain letter called "Big Miss Moviola" (now called "Joanie4Jackie") and asked friends to help distribute pamphlets across the country, which called on female filmmakers to send her their films to be collected and returned in a sort of video mixed tape. "I had this fantasy that I wasn't alone, that there were women and girls all over the country who were also seeking this," she said of its creation. "I think I felt really isolated and poor. I didn't have much of a place in the world yet . . . I was sort of inventing a place for me to be and for women to be." The result was that women filmmakers from all over the country became acquainted and connected with each other's work. Miranda July had created her dream community and went on to write and direct the award-winning film *Me and You and Everyone We Know*, among others.

WHO IS IN YOUR COMMUNITY?

WHO SUPPORTS YOU IN YOUR LIFE?

WHO DO YOU SUPPORT?

WHO IN YOUR LIFE MAKES YOU FEEL INSPIRED, FIRED UP, AND/OR MOST ALIVE?

IF YOU COULD HAVE A PARTY AND INVITE ANYONE LIVING, WHO WOULD IT BE — AND WHY?

IS THERE ANYONE YOU KNOW PERSONALLY WHO COULD ALSO BE DESCRIBED AS YOUR DREAM PARTY GUEST?

Do you have doubts about life? Are you unsure if it is really worth the trouble? ... Stand up and face the east. Now praise the sky and praise the light within each person under the sky. It's okay to be unsure. But praise, praise, praise.

— Miranda July

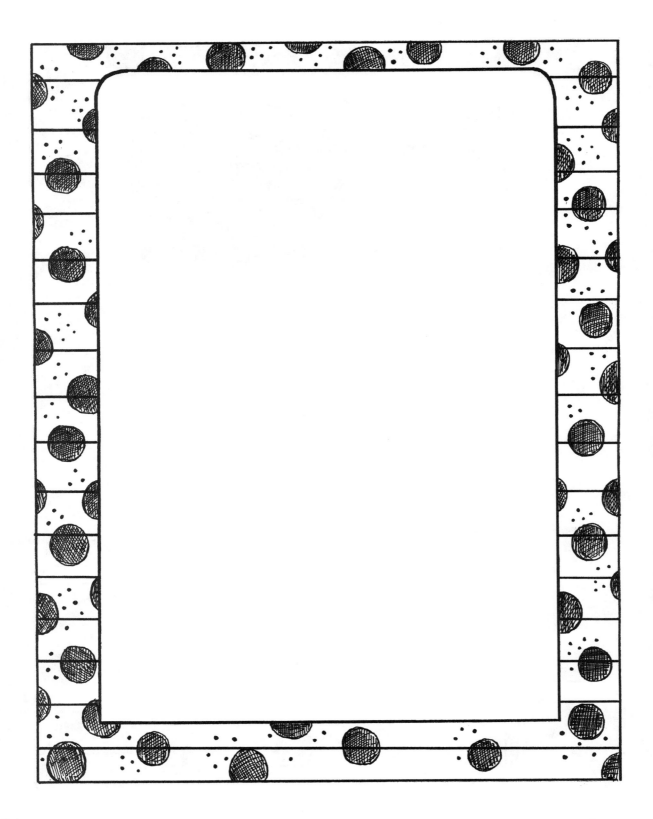

I CANNOT CAUSE LIGHT; THE MOST I CAN DO IS TRY TO PUT MYSELF IN THE PATH OF ITS BEAM.

ANNIE DILLARD

Banana Yoshimoto

Great Gals aim high!

Mahoko Yoshimoto was born in Tokyo in 1964. At the age of five, when she noticed that her sister was good at drawing, she decided she wanted to be equally good at something, so she started writing. Inspired by Stephen King's non-horror stories, she began writing her first novel, *Kitchen*, while working as a waitress in 1987. She took the pen name Banana to remain androgynous, and as she has said, "Just because I love banana flowers." *Kitchen* went on to win numerous awards and become an international sensation. She has written more than twenty books of fiction and nonfiction, many of them global successes. Although she is considered a popular writer, Banana Yoshimoto has received mixed critical reviews, some of which described her work as simplistic and lightweight. Despite this, she has unabashedly said that her ultimate goal is to win the Nobel Prize for Literature. She continues to write in Tokyo.

BUILDING A LAUNCHING PAD

WHERE WOULD YOU LIKE TO BE ONE YEAR FROM NOW?

IN A NEW TOWN? OR A NEW JOB? OR MAYBE SOMETHING
SMALLER - ON VACATION? DREAM BIG OR SMALL!
BRAINSTORM HERE:

**WHAT ARE SOME OF THE STEPS YOU WOULD NEED
TO TAKE TO GET THERE?**

RESEARCH TOWNS, SPRUCE UP YOUR RÉSUMÉ, PRICE AIRLINE
TICKETS. ANY AND ALL ACTIONS!
BRAINSTORM HERE:

CAN YOU BREAK DOWN SOME OF THESE STEPS INTO MONTHLY TASKS?

WHAT CAN YOU DO IN MONTH 1:
WHAT CAN YOU DO IN MONTH 2:
WHAT CAN YOU DO IN MONTH 3:

WHAT CAN YOU DO THIS MONTH?

BRAINSTORM HERE:

WHAT CAN YOU DO TODAY?

BRAINSTORM HERE:

GET READY, GET SET, GO!

The only thing that we should have in mind is not to use our time to fear... There is nobody who has no fear about the future. Thus we should do what we can now, instead of just worrying about the future in vain. — Banana Yoshimoto

" A THOUGHT OCCURRED TO ME TODAY —
SO OBVIOUS, SO ALWAYS OBVIOUS !
IT WAS ABSURD TO SUDDENLY
COMPREHEND IT FOR THE FIRST
TIME — I FELT RATHER GIDDY, A
LITTLE HYSTERICAL : — THERE IS
NOTHING THAT STOPS ME FROM
DOING <u>ANYTHING</u> EXCEPT MYSELF...
WHAT IS TO PREVENT ME FROM
JUST PICKING UP AND TAKING OFF ?
JUST THE <u>SELF</u>-ENFORCED PRESSURES
OF MY ENVIRONMENT, BUT WHICH
HAVE ALWAYS SEEMED SO OMNIPOTENT
THAT I NEVER DARED TO CONTEMPLATE
A VIOLATION OF THEM... GOD, LIVING
IS ENORMOUS ! "

— SUSAN SONTAG

ain't I a woman?

Sojourner Truth

Great Gals are Courageous!

Originally named Isabella Baumfree, Sojourner Truth was born into slavery sometime around 1797 in Swartekill, New York. One of thirteen children, she was sold a number of times until she escaped with her infant daughter. She found refuge with Isaac and Maria Van Wagener, who essentially bought her from her owner until Truth's emancipation came through on July 4, 1827. When she learned that one of her children had been sold illegally, she sought the help of her friends the Van Wageners and took the case to court to free him. In 1829, she moved to New York City and became involved with organizations that worked to support women's rights. After a religious revelation, she took the name Sojourner Truth and traveled as a preacher. She became known as a powerful and compelling speaker and soon began tirelessly speaking out against racism and slavery and for women's rights. Six feet tall and quick-witted, she could be a commanding presence and would never let herself be intimidated. While attending a women's rights conference in 1851, she grew frustrated that no one was addressing the rights of black women. She responded with her powerful and historic speech now known as "Ain't I a Woman?" Truth died in 1883 in her own home, after a lifetime of courageous living.

FINISH THIS SENTENCE:

I have courage because

I am not going to die, I'm going home like a shooting star. - Sojourner Truth

PHYLLIS DILLER!

Great Gals know their material!

Phyllis Ada Diller (née Driver) was born in Lima, Ohio, in 1917. She married early in life and had five children. Diller worked as a secretary and advertising copywriter while caring for her home and kids. When working as a secretary for KGO-TV in San Francisco, local television host Willard Anderson enjoyed her sense of humor so much that he had her on his show. Soon after, her stand-up comedy career was up and running. She went on to deliver jokes about domestic life and self-deprecating portraits of herself on the *Jack Paar Show* and as a contestant on *You Bet Your Life*. She credits Bob Hope for pushing her career further, as he invited her to perform in twenty-three television specials, several films, and a USO tour of Vietnam. Considered to be one of the pioneers in female stand-up comedy, Diller still holds the Guinness world record for delivering the most punch lines in a minute.

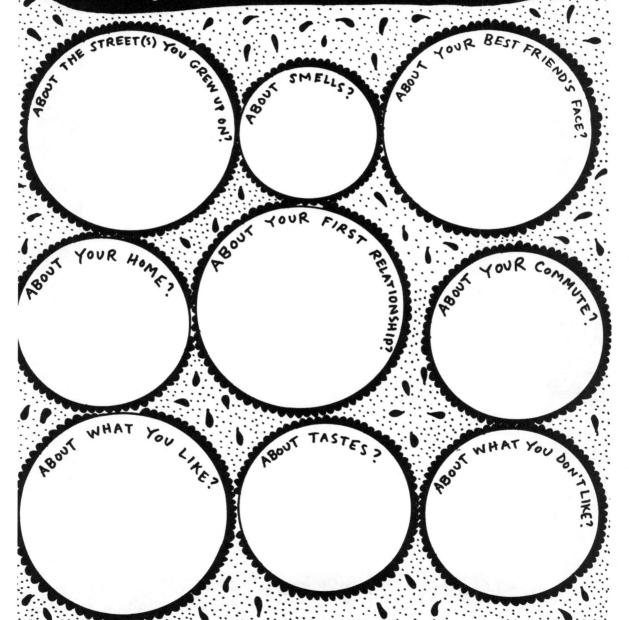

Aim high, and you won't shoot your foot off. - Phyllis Diller

Odetta

Great Gals know who they are!

Odetta Holmes was born in Birmingham, Alabama, in 1930, but grew up in Los Angeles. After discovering that Odetta had a singing voice, her mother had dreams of her taking after the classical opera singer Marian Anderson. She saved enough money for Odetta to receive classical singing lessons from the age of thirteen. But Odetta had other ideas. As she has said, she couldn't see a future for a tall African American girl in opera. In 1949, she joined a national touring company performing in musicals, which led her to San Francisco. It was there, listening to music in the cafés of North Beach, that she decided to try her hand at folk music. With folk legend Pete Seeger's encouragement, Odetta released her first album, *Tin Angel*, in 1954. She is known for her powerful, deep voice and for her presence in the Civil Rights Movement. She received much attention for her performance of "O Freedom" at the 1963 civil rights march to Washington. Martin Luther King Jr. called her the Queen of Folk Music, and her musical influence has spanned from Bob Dylan to Janis Joplin to Steve Earle. She was scheduled to sing at the 2009 Presidential Inauguration, but she died on December 2, 2008, of heart failure. She was seventy-seven.

WHERE DO YOU FEEL IT?
(DRAW A LINE FROM FEELING TO BODY)

SAD

ANGRY

TIRED

WORRY

STRESS

FEAR

HATE

UNINTERESTED

BORED

HAPPY

EXCITED

HOPEFUL

INSPIRED

LOVE

JOY

WONDER

ENERGETIC

CURIOUS

HUNGRY

WHAT DO YOU FEEL RIGHT THIS SECOND?

WHERE DO YOU FEEL IT?

School taught me how to count and taught me how to put a sentence together. But as far as the human spirit goes, I learned through folk music. — ODETTA

Nelle Harper Lee was born in Monroeville, Alabama, in 1926. She studied law but dropped out during her last year. After quitting law school, she moved to New York and worked as an airline reservation clerk, writing in her spare time. After a generous gift from her friends to spend a year writing, she produced the first draft of her novel, *To Kill a Mockingbird*. It would go on to be an immediate bestseller, win the Pulitzer Prize, and be considered one of the greatest American novels of all time. Everyone hotly anticipated what her next book would be, but as it turned out, the waiting would continue. Against expectations, advice, skepticism, and criticism, Lee has yet to publish another novel. You would think this would diminish her notoriety and her books' stature, but it hasn't. Instead, Lee has won prestigious awards for the last forty years and gone on to live a life on her own terms as a reclusive and unapologetic figure.

WHAT RULES DO YOU LIVE BY?

FINISH THESE SENTENCES:

I WILL BE HAPPY WHEN...

I WILL BE CONFIDENT WHEN...

I WILL FEEL FREE WHEN...

Many receive advice, only the wise profit from it. — Harper Lee

POSITIVITY FREE ZONE!

ALERT! **ALERT!**

BECAUSE WE ALL NEED A PLACE TO COMPLAIN, BITCH, YELL, RANT, RAVE, KVETCH, WHINE, FLAIL!

YOU CAN DO IT HERE!

Susan Sontag

Great Gals follow their passions!

Susan Sontag was born in New York City in 1933. She was always precocious, learning to read at age three, graduating from high school at fifteen, and marrying Phillip Rieff, a sociology lecturer at the University of Chicago, when she was just seventeen. By the time she was twenty-four, she had a child, got divorced, moved to Paris, and started having relationships with women. After she returned to the United States to teach philosophy and theology in various academic settings, she quit academia entirely to concentrate fully on writing. In 1963, she published her first novel, *The Benefactor*. While she considered herself primarily a novelist, she was catapulted to fame thanks to her essays on cultural and political matters. She always followed her own interests and took them seriously. As a passionate moviegoer, often seeing two to three movies in a day, she wrote and directed four of her own films in the late 1960s and early '70s. She also wrote and directed several plays, including a production of Beckett's *Waiting for Godot* in Sarajevo during its nearly four-year siege. At the time of her death in 2004, at the age of seventy-one, she was still working and planning new projects.

What are some of your dreams? What would you like to do before you die? Climb Mount Everest? Have a child? Start a list now! You'll be surprised by how quickly they start coming true!

I was not looking for my dreams to interpret my life, but rather for my life to interpret my dreams.
  - Susan Sontag

Great Gals do more than one thing well!

Roberta Joan Anderson was born in Alberta, Canada, in 1943. She grew up drawing with dreams of becoming an artist. Later, in art school, a teacher told her that if she could paint pictures with colors, she could learn to paint them with words as well. So she began to write and play guitar. Through her husband and then music partner, Chuck Mitchell, she started performing in the United States. After their divorce, she performed on her own, gaining notoriety for her beautiful voice and emotionally honest lyrics. Joni Mitchell was the first singer-songwriter to be considered "confessional," which created a devoted fan base of people who strongly identified with her songs. Primarily known as a folk singer, she went on to experiment with both rock music and jazz. During her music career, she continued to paint, contributing art to several of her album covers. Each medium seems to feed the other. She has said, "I have always thought of myself as a painter derailed by circumstance."

UNINSPIRED, BORED, AND AIMLESS

WHAT'S A GAL TO DO?

IDEAS TO BUST YOU OUT! — IDEAS FOR A NEW PERSPECTIVE!

MEND SOCKS, SEW BUTTONS – TEND TO ANYTHING THAT NEEDS MENDING.

PAINT A CHAIR YOUR FAVORITE COLOR – EITHER ONE YOU ALREADY HAVE OR A USED ONE.

GET RID OF CLOTHES, OBJECTS, BOOKS, ANYTHING YOU DON'T USE OR LIKE!

WRITE A LIST OF IDEAS YOU HAVE HAD IN THE PAST BUT HAVEN'T ACTED ON. ANY ONE YOU CAN ACT ON NOW? ACTING ON IDEAS CREATES ROOM FOR MORE IDEAS!

TAKE COLORED CHALK (OR WHITE CHALK IF YOUR WALLS HAVE COLOR) AND WRITE MESSAGES OR WORDS ON YOUR WALLS. YOU CAN WIPE THEM OFF WITH A DAMP CLOTH LATER.

WRITE POSTCARDS TO FAR-FLUNG FRIENDS OR FAMILY – OR EVEN SOMEONE YOU ADMIRE – AND MAIL THEM!

WHEN ALL ELSE FAILS, GO FOR A WALK

At the point where I'm trying to force something and it's not happening, and I'm getting frustrated with, say, writing a poem, I can go and pick up the brushes and start painting. At the point where the painting seems to not be going anywhere, I go and pick up the guitar.
— Joni Mitchell

YOUR LIFE, YOUR ACHIEVEMENT, YOUR HAPPINESS, YOUR PERSON ARE OF PARAMOUNT IMPORTANCE. LIVE UP TO YOUR HIGHEST VISION OF YOURSELF NO MATTER WHAT THE CIRCUMSTANCES YOU MIGHT ENCOUNTER.

AYN RAND

JOAN JETT

Great Gals work on their own behalf!

Joan Marie Larkin was born near Philadelphia in 1958. Her family relocated to the West Coast when she was thirteen. At age fifteen, she cofounded the all-girl rock band the Runaways. After the Runaways disbanded, Jett went on to a solo career, cowriting and producing with her pal Kenny Laguna her self-titled debut in 1980. After the album was rejected by twenty-three record labels, Jett and Laguna released it on their own label, Blackheart Records, went on tour, and sold the album out of the back of their car. Eventually, the album would be picked up by Boardwalk Records and released as *Bad Reputation*, launching Jett's solo career into superstardom. With the enormous success of her follow-up effort, *I Love Rock 'n' Roll*, Jett set the standard for female rock musicians for decades to come. She continues to rock the world as a performer, producer, and outspoken activist.

What Can You Do?

MAKE YOUR OWN LUCK! ♥ YOUR TIMING IS PERFECT!

THERE IS ALWAYS SOMETHING YOU CAN DO ON YOUR OWN BEHALF.

IS THERE SOMETHING YOU WOULD LIKE TO DO?

WRITE A BOOK? STUDY GORILLAS IN THE JUNGLE? TRAVEL AROUND THE WORLD? CHANGE CAREERS? WRITE IT HERE:

IS THERE ONE SMALL ACTION YOU CAN TAKE TOWARD THIS IDEA?

WRITE FOR 15 MINUTES? LOOK UP GORILLA PROGRAMS? INVESTIGATE AROUND THE WORLD FARES? CALL OR E-MAIL SOMEONE WHO HAS THE CAREER YOU WANT?

WRITE IT HERE:

REMINDERS:
SOMETIMES WHEN WE GET STUCK AND DON'T TAKE
ACTION WE FEEL LIKE VICTIMS OF OUR PLIGHT.
DON'T WAIT TO "GET READY" (YOU'RE READY NOW!);
STOP WAITING ON OTHERS TO RESPOND OR CALL YOU
BACK (TAKE A DIFFERENT ROUTE!); STOP THINKING
"MAYBE LATER" (LATER IS NOW!); THE NEXT TIME
SOMEONE TELLS YOU (OR YOU TELL YOURSELF) "IT
CAN'T BE DONE" REPLY WITH: THEN WHY DO OTHERS
DO IT? EVEN IF IT'S ONE SMALL ACTION - TAKE IT!
YOU CAN ALWAYS DO SOMETHING TOWARD IT!

IDEAS · IDEAS · IDEAS · IDEAS · IDEAS ·

I think I was born strong-willed. That's not the kind of thing you can learn. The advantage is, you stick to what you believe in and rarely get pushed out of what you want to do.
    — Joan Jett

You Are Your own Promised Land, your own new frontier.
— Julia Cameron

Great Gals are determined!

Writer and activist Alice Walker was born the eighth child of a sharecropping family in Georgia in 1944. Her intelligence and determination were detected early, when, despite an accident that left her blinded in one eye, she went on to graduate as valedictorian of her high school. Through scholarships, she was able to attend Spelman College and Sarah Lawrence College, where she graduated in 1965. She began her activism by working at the voter turn-out drives in Georgia and for welfare rights in New York City. She published her first book of poems, *Once*, in 1968, with the help of her mentor, the poet Muriel Rukeyser. The author of more than thirty books of poetry, fiction, and nonfiction, Walker is best known for her novel *The Color Purple*, which won the Pulitzer Prize in 1983. A continuing activist, she has spoken out for environmental and women's rights. She is also responsible for the resurrection of published works by writer Zora Neale Hurston, and for paying for a gravestone to mark the late Hurston's grave. She continues to inspire generations of women with her steadfast determination in all that she creates.

I DARE YOU!

FOR ONE DAY DO NOT GOSSIP.

WRITE A LIST OF POSITIVE ATTRIBUTES ABOUT SOMEONE YOU HAVE DIFFICULTY WITH.

SPEND NO MONEY FOR ONE DAY.

COMPLIMENT A COMPLETE STRANGER.

Don't wait around for other people to be happy for you. Any happiness you get you've got to make yourself.
 - Alice Walker

Great Gals dance to their own beat!

Martha Graham was seventeen when she saw a dance performance by Ruth St. Denis. As she said, "That night my fate was sealed." She studied theater and dance for the next twelve years, developing her expressive and unique gift for telling stories through dance. In 1926, she opened her own school of contemporary dance and began to create ballets concerned with social and political issues. She caused a stir when she refused an invitation to participate in the Berlin Olympic Games of 1936. She conceived entirely every ballet her company performed, down to choreography, costumes, and music. As a result, the performances always had a very distinct style both physically and aesthetically. Throughout her career she would create 181 ballets, perform for seven presidents, and create a style of dancing whose far-reaching influence continues to be studied to this day. She stopped dancing at age seventy-six, but choreographed and worked on dance projects until her death at ninety-six.

HOW ARE YOU DIFFERENT

FROM YOUR FAMILY?

FROM YOUR COWORKERS?

FROM YOUR FRIENDS?

I wanted to begin not with characters or ideas, but with movements... I wanted significant movement. I did not want it to be beautiful or fluid. I wanted it to be fraught with inner meaning, with excitement and surge. —Martha Graham

TO FREE US FROM
THE EXPECTATIONS
OF OTHERS, TO
GIVE US BACK TO
OURSELVES — THERE
LIES THE GREAT,
SINGULAR POWER
OF SELF-RESPECT.
— JOAN DIDION

FRIDA KAHLO

Great Gals draw from experience!

Frida Kahlo was born to Matilde and Guillermo Kahlo in Coyoacán, Mexico, in 1907. Her father was a photographer who doted on her and encouraged her artistic talents. When she was eighteen, she was involved in a horrific traffic accident that left her with debilitating injuries. While she endured many surgeries and recuperated, she began to paint, beginning with a self-portrait as a letter to her absent boyfriend. The relation to painting, love, and physical hardship would be a continuing pattern for the rest of her life. When she was twenty-two, she married the painter Diego Rivera, who was known for his passion of Mexico, politics, painting, and women. He and Kahlo would have a stormy relationship, filled with affairs, miscarriages, divorce, and eventual remarriage. Her powerful self-portraits, still lifes, and portraits of friends and family depict what was familiar and dear to her. Often surrealistic yet painfully frank about her own physical and emotional suffering, her work urged the artist André Breton to call her paintings "a ribbon around a bomb." She remains a reigning icon of art.

Life Notes

LIFE ENLARGES, LIFE TAKES AIM. – ANNE SEXTON

IN THE LAST 3 MONTHS:

WHAT MOVIES HAVE YOU SEEN?

WHAT BOOKS HAVE YOU READ?

WHAT PEOPLE HAVE YOU SEEN?

HOURS WORKED?

TRIPS TAKEN?

THINGS STARTED.

TV SHOWS WATCHED?

THINGS BOUGHT?

THINGS FINISHED?

THINGS EATEN?

WHAT WOULD YOU LIKE TO DO IN THE NEXT 3?

WHO WOULD YOU LIKE TO SEE? WHERE WOULD YOU LIKE TO GO? WHAT GOALS WOULD YOU LIKE TO MEET? HOW DO YOU WANT TO SPEND YOUR TIME? THINK BIG! THINK SMALL!

I paint my own reality. The only thing I know is that I paint because I need to, and I paint whatever passes through my head without any other consideration. - Frida Kahlo

Fling yourself
in the flow.
Don't be afraid.
The whole logic
of the universe
is contained in
daring. — Erica Jong

Margaret Sanger

Great Gals stand up for what they believe in!

Margaret Sanger was born in Corning, New York, in 1879. Growing up in a Roman Catholic household, Sanger witnessed firsthand the physical strain a lifetime of pregnancies took on her own mother. Her mother, who had eighteen pregnancies and eleven live births, would eventually die of complications due to tuberculosis and cervical cancer. Working as a nurse and midwife on the Lower East Side of New York furthered her belief that pregnancy and childbirth, wanted or not, took a toll on women's health. She saw women weakened and killed by too many pregnancies, unable to care for the children they already had, and without any aid or knowledge of how to change their circumstances. She came to believe that education and control of one's fertility were essential to ensure the well-being and rights of women. Against a firestorm of controversy, Sanger was the first to set up education centers and to distribute contraception. She risked imprisonment, physical harm, and personal losses to further the cause of reproductive rights for women. As Gloria Steinem said of her, "She taught us, first, to look at the world as if women mattered." She worked for the reproductive rights of women until her death in 1966 at the age of eighty-six.

WHAT DO YOU BELIEVE IN?

I BELIEVE IN MAKING THINGS FROM SCRATCH · I BELIEVE IN ADMITTING WHEN YOU'RE WRONG · I BELIEVE IN WRITING LETTERS · I BELIEVE IN GIVING FOOD INSTEAD OF MONEY TO PANHANDLERS · I BELIEVE IN SINGING LOUDLY IN THE CAR · I BELIEVE IN BOOKSTORES · I BELIEVE IN YOU

Woman must not accept; she must challenge. She must not be awed by that which has been built up around her; she must reverence that woman in her which struggles for expression.
— Margaret Sanger

Great Gals are daydreamers!

Sandra Cisneros was born in Chicago in 1954, the only daughter out of seven children. As a child, she struggled in school and her teachers labeled her a daydreamer. She has said that this caused her to retreat into her own imagination and to believe she wasn't smart as a child. In high school, she found a teacher who recognized her artistic talents and encouraged her. She began to write poetry and became the school's literary magazine editor. While in graduate school for poetry at the University of Iowa, she began the early drafts of what would become her first novel, *The House on Mango Street*. It went on to win numerous awards and is now taught in many high school curriculums. It was only when she received a MacArthur Fellowship (known as the Genius Award) at the age of forty that she realized how much being a daydreamer had helped her. She has written, "What [the award] finally made me realize was this: I have always been a daydreamer and that's a lucky thing for a writer because what is a daydreamer if not another word for thinker, visionary, dreamer—all wonderful words synonymous with *girl*." Her award-winning works include two poetry collections, a short story collection, and the novel *Caramelo*.

USE THIS SPACE AS A RESPONSIBLE-FREE ZONE!

FINISH THESE SENTENCES:

I DREAM OF BECOMING...

I DREAM OF HAVING...

I DREAM OF KNOWING...

I was silent as a child, and silenced as a young woman; I am taking my lumps and bumps for being a big mouth now, but usually from those whose opinions I don't respect. — Sandra Cisneros

May Sarton

Great Gals keep going!

The only child of a science historian and an artist, May Sarton was born in Belgium in 1912 and grew up in Boston, Massachusetts. She received a scholarship to attend Vassar but turned it down to pursue her passion for the theater. She also began to write poems, publishing several in *Poetry* magazine when she was just seventeen. After a failed attempt at starting her own theater company, she turned her back on the theater permanently for a career in writing. For the next sixty years, she wrote and produced more than forty published works, including poetry, fiction, and memoirs. Her work was generally well received, garnering a National Book Award nomination for both fiction and poetry, and Sarton never stopped producing work, regardless of time or fashion. Some of her most successful works were published in her later life, including her landmark journals *Plant Dreaming Deep* and *Journal of a Solitude*. Coinciding with the feminist movement, these works are considered seminal in advancing women's autobiography and have inspired generations of readers in their passion and their honesty. Through the next decade her popularity soared and her productivity never wearied. Sarton would live into her eighties, writing her last book of memoirs, *At Eighty-Two: A Journal*, in the last year of her life.

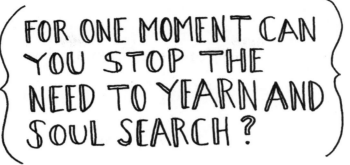

What if you had already reached the peak of yourself?

Then what?

What if this was all the love you were going to get?

Then what?

What if this was all there was ever going to be?

Then what?

What if there was nothing left to improve?   **Then what?**

What if there was nothing more to be done?   **Then what?**

What if there was just this moment?   **Then what?**

Each day, and the living of it, has to be a conscious creation in which discipline and order are relieved with some play and pure foolishness. — May Sarton

Write Your Own Afterword

THIS IS YOUR BOOK, YOUR STORY, YOUR LIFE

ANY CLOSING THOUGHTS?

PUT YOUR
MOTTO,
FAVORITE
QUOTE, ETC.
HERE

START WITH THIS PHRASE IF YOU NEED HELP:

IT WAS A TIME WHEN...

I LIKE LIVING. I HAVE SOMETIMES BEEN WILDLY, DESPAIR-INGLY, ACUTELY MISERABLE, RACKED WITH SORROW, BUT THROUGH IT ALL I STILL KNOW QUITE CERTAINLY THAT JUST TO BE ALIVE IS A GRAND THING. — AGATHA CHRISTIE

It Was Perfect

By now you are probably on to something different than you were when you first decided to use this book. Or maybe you turned to this page directly from the beginning and are reading these last words the first time you open the book (that would be me). There is something so sweet about a finished story. We have witnessed the fragile beginning, the trial of effort, and now the triumphant finish. A book is done, the sun sets, the credits roll, and the music soars. Movies bank on this. Biographies and memoirs fly off the shelves because of this.

But in truth, life isn't so clean-cut. Sure, it can be triumphant, but it can also be boring. It can be aimless, seemingly without point or context. Then you look back, and you see it was perfect anyway. Does it matter any less in the moment? No, it doesn't. It's your life you are spending, and as the writer Annie Dillard once said, "Spend an afternoon. Spend it all—you can't take it with you."

So spend what you have, which is your greatness. The greatness is not in accomplishing great things; the greatness is in living as you really are. Stay in bed all day and question everything, start a new project, quit a job, become famous to a select few, go to Paris, or stay at home. Only you can write your life story and at the end, what do you think mattered: the fact that you existed or the fact that you *lived*? So keep going. Keep living your one, great life.

—THANK YOU—

TO THE TEAM OF GREAT GALS WHO MADE THIS BOOK HAPPEN: MY ROCK STAR AGENT, DANIELLE SVETCOV! MY MULTITALENTED EDITORS, MARIA GAGLIANO & MEG LEDER

TO EVERYONE WHO BOUGHT THE ORIGINAL GREAT GAL CALENDARS 2001-2008

TO NIKKI HARDIN AND ALL AT SKIRT! MAGAZINE WHERE "EVERYDAY ACTS OF POWER," "HOW TO TURN YOUR HOME INTO A RETREAT," "OH FOR THE LOVE OF YOU," "RESOLUTION REVOLUTION," "BREAK-A-RULE," "WALKING LIFE," AND "SECRET AGENT FOR GOOD" FIRST APPEARED.

TO THE READERS OF MY BLOG AN ACCIDENT OF HOPE www.summerpierre.com

TO MY FAMILY + FRIENDS - ESPECIALLY ALL THE GREAT WOMEN IN MY LIFE WHO MAKE ME LAUGH AND INSPIRE GREATNESS!

MOST OF ALL THANK YOU TO MY TWO GREAT GUYS: — GRAHAM and GUS —
who gave me time and space to create this book and who make my life amazingly GREAT!

Summer Pierre is the author of *The Artist in the Office: How to Creatively Survive and Thrive Seven Days a Week*. She lives a great life in Brooklyn, New York, with her family. Visit her website at www.summerpierre.com.